SAFARI CREATURES

SAFARI CREATURES

Sujatha Menon

PowerKiDS
press.

New York

Published in 2008 by The Rosen Publishing Group, Inc.
29 East 21st Street, New York, NY 10010

First Published: 2006
Designed by Q2A Media

Picture credits:
l: Left, r: Right, t: Top, b: Bottom, c: Center

6t: Boleslaw Kubica, 8t: Laurin Rinder, 8c: Anna de'Capitani d'Arzago Photography,
9t: J. Norman Reid, 9b: Daniel Bellhouse, 10: Stuart Taylor, 11: Keith Levit,
14bl: Todd Hackwelder, 14br: Chris Fourie, 14-15c: Timothy Passmore, 15b: Neil Wigmore,
16t: Brad Thompson, 16b: Sarah Spencer, 17b: Vladimir Pomortzeff,
18-19b: Johan Swanepoel, 19t: Xavier Marchant, 20t: Susan Adams,
20c: EcoPrint, 20-21b: Courtesy of Carnegie Museum of Natural History,
22b: EcoPrint, 23t: Tom Graham Photography, 23b: Anna de'Capitani d'Arzago Photography,
24-25b: Bananaman, 26l: Scott Sanders, 27cr: Xavier Marchant,
27b: Petri Aukia, 28-29c: EcoPrint, 30t: Anna de'Capitani d'Arzago Photography,
30cl & 30b: EcoPrint, 31t: Kirk Peart Professional Imaging, 32-33tc: Taolmor,
33t: Bart Coessens, 34t: Johan Swanepoel, 34bl: Koval, 34-35bc: Patrick Hermans,
36t & 36-37b: Smeyf, 38tr: SI, 38-39b: EcoPrint, 39r: Tad Denson, 40t: Ilya D. Gridnev,
40-41b: Ruslan, 41t: Gertfrik, 42-43t: Gavriel Jecan

Library of Congress Cataloging-in-Publication Data

Menon, Sujatha.
  Safari creatures / Sujatha Menon.
    p. cm. — (Wild creatures)
  Includes index.
  ISBN-13: 978-1-4042-3894-7 (library binding)
  ISBN-10: 1-4042-3894-8 (libray binding)
  1. Savanna animals—Juvenile literature. I. Title.
  QL115.3.M46 2007
  591.74'8—dc22

                                                2007008672

Manufactured in China

CONTENTS

LIFE IN THE SAVANNAHS

The African savannah offers the best safari because it is teeming with animals and there are not many trees to block the view.

Most of us would love to go on a safari to see wild animals in their natural habitat. The best place for that would be a savannah. A savannah is a large area of land filled with tall grass and very few trees. Savannahs are also known as tropical grasslands and are found on the edges of rainforests. They cover parts of India, Australia, South America and almost half of Africa.

Weather watch

Savannahs are warm throughout the year. Temperatures vary between 68° F and 86° F (20° C–30° C). There are only two seasons in the savannahs, a dry winter season that lasts from four to six months and a wet summer season that lasts for about eight months. Most savannahs receive a lot of rain during the summer. It can get very hot and humid during these months. The dry winter months are much cooler, but are marked by drought and fire. Wildfires are necessary to maintain the savannahs, because otherwise the trees would multiply and ultimately cover the grasslands.

Fires are necessary to the savannahs, but they must not get out of control.

Plants of the savannahs

Savannahs are dominated by tall grasses, such as star grass, lemon grass, Rhodes grass, elephant grass and shrubs. Savannah grasses are usually coarse and grow in tufts with bare ground in between. Trees can be seen scattered around the region. African savannahs are characterized by the presence of baobab and acacia trees.

Animals of the savannahs

It is interesting to watch several types of animals moving about together in the African savannah.

More than 40 types of hooved mammals, such as antelope, zebras, hippopotamuses, rhinoceroses and giraffes inhabit the savannahs. Around two million herbivores and about 500 species of birds live in the Serengeti Plains of eastern Africa alone. Apart from the plant-eaters, savannahs are also home to large carnivores such as lions, cheetahs, leopards, hyenas and wild dogs. A huge variety of reptiles can also be found here.

Savannah survival tricks

Savannahs are dry regions with very limited water resources during winter months. The plants and animals living in these regions are specially adapted to deal with water shortage. Savannah grasses make the most of the wet season and grow quickly. During the dry season, these grasses turn brown to reduce water loss. The necessary water is stored in the roots and used up in small quantities through the dry season. Baobab trees produce leaves only in the wet season. They also store water in their huge trunks and use that water through the dry season. The acacia has long taproots that can reach water deep in the ground. Some animals remain in their burrows throughout the dry season, while others migrate. Most savannah animals can run quite fast, an adaptation that helps them survive wildfires.

Giraffes graze on the tops of acacia trees, resulting in their umbrella-shaped tops.

KING OF THE SAVANNAHS

The lion is known as the "king of beasts" for a good reason. It is the most majestic and powerful of all cats. Its loud roar reflects its immense strength.

The African lion has a bigger mane and is more majestic in appearance than its Asian cousin.

Life in the savannahs

Lions are usually found in the open grasslands. They are not found in deserts or thick forests. Their brownish yellow coat helps lions to blend into their surroundings. However, the male lion's magnificent mane gives it away. This is one of the reasons why male lions are not as successful at hunting as lionesses. There are two kinds of lions, African and Asiatic. The African lion is found in the African savannahs, while the Asiatic lion is limited to the Gir Forests of western India, in the state of Gujarat.

The mane story

The male lion is the only big cat with a mane. It uses its mane to attract female lions and to scare its competitors. The color and size of the mane determines the lion's strength. Lions with darker and longer manes are more mature and stronger than those with lighter and shorter ones. However, the thick mane exposes the lion to its prey when it hunts. It also increases the body temperature of the lion, making it uncomfortable at times for the animal in its warm habitat.

Built for power

The lion is known for its strength rather than its speed. A lion can run fast, but prefers to creep up on its prey. If the prey senses the presence of its enemy and runs, the lion chases it. However, a lion cannot chase its prey for too long. Prey that can run fast often survives the chase. Lionesses do most of the hunting, with the lion pitching in once in a while. A lion can single-handedly bring down animals as big as a buffalo. However, lionesses are not as strong and therefore hunt in groups, sometimes chasing prey towards the lion.

Male lions are stronger than lionesses, but lionesses are better hunters.

Here is a group of lionesses and cubs at a watering hole.

CREATURE PROFILE

Common name:	Lion
Scientific name:	*Panthera leo*
Found in:	Central Africa and Gir Forest in India
Size:	Adult males: 330–550 pounds (150–250 kg)
	Adult females: 257–370 pounds (117–167 kg)
Prey:	Wildebeest, warthogs, buffalo, zebra, antelope, giraffe and occasionally carrion
Enemies:	Humans. Lions are hunted for their skin, manes and sometimes even for sport.
Status:	Endangered. There are only about 300 Asiatic lions and about 30,000 African lions in the wild.

Social life

Lions are the only big cats that live in groups. A family of lions is called a pride. It consists of about two lions, seven lionesses and several cubs. However, a pride may have as many as 40 lions, lionesses and cubs. The lionesses in a pride are often related to one another. Female cubs continue to live in the pride they are born into, but male cubs leave when they are about three years old. They wander about until they take over another pride.

An angry lion is among the most dangerous animals in the world.

LEOPARD

Leopards are the third largest of the big cats, after tigers and lions. They are excellent climbers and spend most of their time up in trees. They are also extremely adaptable and can live in a wide range of habitats ranging from the African savannahs to the thick forests of Asia.

A leopard drags its kill up the branches of a tree.

Spotted wonder

The leopard is best known for the dark rosette markings on its light tan-colored coat. The spots provide the cat with excellent camouflage in a wide range of habitats. The spots are especially helpful when the leopard is up a tree because they help to hide it well against the branches.

Cheetah Skin

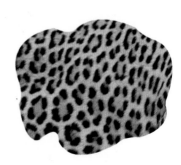

Leopard Skin

Jaguar Skin

Arboreal life

Leopards love to climb trees. They spend a large part of their lives in the treetops. These cats even carry their prey up the trees so that they can eat in peace. This way they are able to stop hyenas from stealing their kill. Leopards have powerful shoulder and chest muscles that help them to drag prey three times their size up a tree.

Skilled hunters

Like all other big cats, leopards prefer to ambush their prey instead of chasing it. The leopard hides in grass or bush and when the prey comes close enough, it launches an attack by leaping on it. Sometimes, leopards stalk monkeys in trees and will even jump down on prey from the branches of a tree. Leopards usually hunt at night, although some female leopards with cubs prefer to hunt during the day. They eat a variety of prey like giraffes, jackals, antelope and birds.

The agile leopard is one of the cleverest hunters in the wild.

CREATURE PROFILE

Common name:	Leopard
Scientific name:	*Panthera pardus*
Found in:	West and South Africa, Middle East, India, Pakistan, Nepal, Java, Sri Lanka, China, Siberia and most of Southeast Asia
Size:	Adult males: 65–155 pounds (30–70 kg)
	Adult females: 45–110 pounds (20–50 kg)
Prey:	Giraffe, monkey, jackal, antelope, and any other animal it can get its claws into
Enemies:	Humans. Leopards are hunted for their skin and for sport. Sometimes they are also killed to protect livestock.
Status:	Most of the subspecies are listed endangered. The Amur leopard of Siberia is the most endangered, with hardly 50 individuals existing today.

CHEETAH

The cheetah is a unique member of the cat family. It is the only cat that, while hunting, regularly relies on speed rather than stealth. The cheetah is the fastest animal on land over short distances. The magnificent cheetah can reach speeds of about 70 miles per hour (113 km/h)!

You can always a spot a cheetah by those telltale marks around its nose.

Not a big cat?

The cheetah is commonly referred to as a big cat. However, unlike the true big cats, such as lions and tigers, cheetahs cannot roar. Instead, they purr like domestic cats. Cheetahs are also much smaller in size and are diurnal. They rely on sight and not smell while hunting. The cheetah is the only cat with semiretractable claws. This means their claws are only partially withdrawn in the paw. Despite these differences, the cheetah is often regarded as the smallest member of the big cat family.

Built for speed

Every part of the cheetah's body is adapted for speed. The cat has a narrow, lightweight body with long, slender legs and a flexible spine. It also has a small head, a flat face and enlarged nostrils that help the cat to breathe in more air while running. It also has a powerful heart, enlarged lungs and an oversized liver. The cheetah's strong paws give it a good grip on the ground. The long, muscular tail of the cheetah helps the cat to keep its balance, especially when making quick turns.

When the cheetah sprints, its spine acts like a huge spring, helping it to gain speed.

A cheetah runs down its prey and makes a kill.

CREATURE PROFILE

Common name:	Cheetah
Scientific name:	*Acinonyx jubatus*
Found in:	Africa and Iran
Total length of the body:	45-55 inches (112-135 cm)
Tail length:	26-33 inches (65-84 cm)
Prey:	Wildebeest, gazelles, impalas and other small, hooved animals
Enemies:	Lions, hyenas and humans
Status:	Threatened. Fewer than 12,500 cheetahs remain in the wild today.

The price of speed

The cheetah's speed is also one of its biggest disadvantages. Although it can run at high speeds, the cheetah cannot maintain that speed for more than 1,476 feet (450 m). This is because running at such a high speed causes the cheetah's body temperature to increase so much that it may become fatal. This is why cheetahs do not engage in long chases. The cat usually catches its prey within a minute. It trips its prey during the chase and then bites on the throat to suffocate it. The cheetah's small teeth and weak jaws make it impossible for the cat to break its prey's neck.

Female cheetahs prefer to live alone except when they raise their cubs.

Social life

Male cheetahs are very social. They live together in small groups that usually consist of brothers from the same litter. Female cheetahs, however, prefer to live alone. A female cheetah looks after her cubs all by herself. When the young cheetahs are about 18 months old, the mother leaves them. The group of cubs continue to live together until the female cubs are old enough to leave the group. The males remain together for life.

ELEPHANT

Elephants are the world's largest land animals. They are bulky and strong and have no natural predators. There are two kinds of elephants — the African and Asian.

Size matters

The African and Asian species are very different from each other. Both have distinct features and are easily identified. The African species are much larger than their Asian relatives. They also have less hair on the body. However, the most distinguishing feature of the African elephant is its huge, fan-shaped ears. Moreover, both male and female African elephants have tusks, whereas only the males of Asian elephants have tusks.

Note the many differences between Asian (left) and African (right) elephant.

Of tusks and trunk

The trunk is a combination of the nose and the upper lip. The elephant uses its strong, flexible trunk to carry objects, break off branches and pluck leaves. It is also used to drink water. The nostrils at the tip of the trunk help to smell. The elephant waves its trunk about to capture a scent. The trunk is then placed in the mouth so that special organs can identify the scent. The tusks are actually elongated incisor teeth. They are used for various purposes, from digging for food and water to territorial fights and defense.

P.O. BOX 250
RUSHFORD, MN 55971

 *A herd of Asian elephants approaches a watering hole.*

Living together

Elephants are highly social animals. They live in large groups called herds, consisting of about 30 elephants. A herd is comprised of female elephants and their young ones. The members of a herd are very close to one another and are led by the oldest female elephant. They eat, bathe and migrate together. They also move about as a group and stay close to their leader. The healthier elephants take care of the young, sick and old members of the herd. When threatened, the leader leads the herd in a stampede.

Aggressive males

Adult male elephants are not allowed to live in the herd they are born into. When they are old enough to mate, young males either leave the herd or are driven out by adult females. These outcasts usually wander off alone or join a group of other young males forming bachelor herds. Male elephants are very aggressive. Solitary males are especially dangerous as they sometimes attack without warning. Males of a bachelor herd often fight one another.

The elephant that wins the fight is allowed to join a herd and breed.

CREATURE PROFILE

Common name:	African Elephant
Scientific name:	*Loxodonta africana*
Found in:	Sub-Saharan Africa
Size:	Weight: 15,000–20,000 pounds (7,000–10,000 kg)
	Height: 10–11.5 feet (3–3.5 m)
Feed on:	Branches and leaves
Enemies:	Humans. Elephants are killed for their tusks.
Status:	African elephants are considered to be threatened.

RHINOCEROS

The rhinoceros is a hooved mammal that is found in parts of Asia and Africa. There are five species of rhinoceros: the Sumatran, Javan, Indian, and the white and black rhinos of Africa.

Common features

The different species of rhinoceros have some features in common. They have thick skin with folds. They also have short, thick legs and a tiny tail. Most rhino species have one large horn above the nose with a smaller one behind it. All rhinos prefer to live alone and come together only during the mating season. Mother rhinos stay with their calves until they are old enough to take care of themselves.

This is a two-horned rhino with her calf.

The Javan rhino is the rarest of the rhino species.

The Asian rhinos

The Indian rhinoceros, or the great one-horned rhino, is the most numerous of the three Asian species. It is found in Nepal and the state of Assam in India. Each Asian species has unique features. The Indian and Javan rhinos have only one horn, while the Sumatran species, the smallest of all, is the only rhino with thick fur. The Sumatran and Javan species are the most endangered of all rhinos. There are only about 100 Javan and 300 Sumatran rhinos in the world today.

The African rhinos

The white rhino is also known as the square-lipped rhino. It is found in northeastern and southern Africa. This species has a wide mouth that helps it to cut grass. It has two horns on its snout and a hump on the back of its neck. Compared to the white rhino, its black counterpart is smaller and does not have a hump on the neck. The black rhino has a pointed, prehensile upper lip that is ideal for grabbing leaves.

The square-lipped white rhino has a characteristic hump on its neck.

The demand for their horns is what endangers the rhino.

CREATURE PROFILE

Common name:	Black rhinoceros
Scientific name:	*Diceros bicornis*
Found in:	Eastern and Central Africa
Height:	4.5–5.5 feet (1.4–1.7 m)
Weight:	1,700–3,000 pounds (800 –1,400 kg)
Feed on:	Leaves and twigs
Enemies:	Humans. Black rhinos are poached for their horns.
Status:	Endangered. Hardly 3,500 black rhinos exist today.

Priceless horns

All five species of rhinos are endangered, because they were once hunted extensively for their horns. The Indian and the white rhino populations have shown a marked improvement following conservation efforts. However, the Javan, Sumatran and black rhinos are not recovering. Rhino horns are used in traditional Asian medicine to counter some poisons. Rhino horns were also used to make handles for daggers and other expensive objects.

HIPPOPOTAMUS

Hippopotamus means "river horse" in Greek. The hippopotamus belongs to a group of hooved mammals called artiodactyls. The animals in this group have either two toes or four toes. The Hippopotamus has four toes. It is a plant-eating, water-loving giant.

Hippo facts

Hippopotamuses are found only in parts of Africa. There are two species of hippopotamus, the common and the pygmy hippopotamus. The common hippopotamus is one of the largest land mammals. It is around 5 feet (1.5 m) tall and weighs about 8,800 pounds (4,000 kg). The pygmy hippopotamus, on the other hand, is only 30 inches (75 cm) tall and weighs about 400 pounds (180 kg).

In the mornings and evenings, the hippos come out of water to graze.

Adapted for water

Pygmy hippos prefer to stay near water rather than in it. Common hippos, however, spend a great deal of time wallowing in water. They usually spend their days in water, and come out in the morning and at nights to feed. Their eyes are positioned on top of the head. This helps to keep the eyes above the water when the hippo is submerged. Its nostrils are sealed whenever it dives underwater. Hippos can remain submerged for up to half an hour, though they prefer not to stay submerged for more than about five minutes.

Natural sunscreen!

The skin of a hippo has very little hair. Common hippos have coppery-brown skin, while pygmy hippos are greenish-black. The pores in the skin of a common hippo secrete a reddish-pink fluid. It is referred to as "blood sweat", but is neither blood nor sweat. The fluid consists of red and orange pigments. Both pigments act as sunscreen lotion, absorbing harmful ultraviolet rays and preventing the skin from cracking in the heat.

CREATURE PROFILE

Common name:	Common hippopotamus
Scientific name:	*Hippopotamus amphibius*
Found in:	Central, western and southern Africa
Size:	Weight: 3,300–8,800 pounds (1,500–4,000 kg) Length: 11 feet (3.5 m)
Feed on:	Grass, leaves and other vegetation
Enemies:	Humans. Hunting and habitat loss are the major threats to hippopotamus populations.
Status:	Threatened

The red pigment also protects the hippo from disease-causing bacteria.

Hippo behavior

Hippos live in herds. The number of hippos in a herd ranges from 10 to 20. They are highly territorial and will fiercely defend their herd. Male hippos mark their territory along the riverbanks and defend it against other males. They usually threaten each other by opening their mouths wide and showing off their large canine teeth. Male hippos often use their huge, strong heads as weapons when fighting with each other over territory.

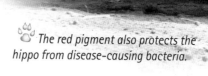
Male hippos can be very aggressive when protecting their territory.

ANTELOPE

The term "antelope" is used to refer to a group of plant-eating hooved mammals that are related to cattle and goats. There are at least 90 varieties of antelope. The smallest of these is the royal antelope, while the giant eland is the largest species.

🐾 *The giant eland is the largest antelope.*

Common features

🐾 *The gemsbok oryx has a pair of distinctive spearlike horns.*

All antelope have light, slender bodies covered with thick, short fur. Most antelope are sandy brown, but there are exceptions such as the gemsbok, which has gray and black fur. They have cloven hooves and short tails. They have strong hindquarters, long legs and powerful muscles, that help them run fast. Running antelope look as if they are bouncing up and down. Antelope are also excellent jumpers, but not good at climbing. Both male and female of most antelope species grow horns. The male's horns are typically larger.

Sensing danger

Antelope are highly alert creatures. They have keen senses that help them identify danger early. Their elongated pupils give antelope a broad view of their surroundings. Their senses of hearing and smell are also excellent, helping the animals to sense danger even in the dark. They usually warn one another with various calls. Some antelope bounce up and down, keeping their legs straight. This display is known as "stotting" or "pronking."

Running for life

The antelope's speed is their weapon against predators. Antelope usually flee when alarmed. However, the choice of when to flee is dependent on the type of predator and its distance from the herd. They let lions come within 219 yards (200 m) and then run, while they run when a cheetah is 875 yards (800 m) away. Antelope can make quick, sharp turns and run fast for a long period. This is a huge advantage, especially when chased by a cheetah, as the cat cannot run at its top speed for very long.

The male antelope fight fiercely during the mating season.

Locking horns

A herd of antelope escapes from a cheetah.

Horns form a major part of an antelope's social life. They are extremely important during mating displays and leadership fights. Male antelope are territorial and often fight with each other for control of the herd. Each species of antelope has a different way of fighting, but all antelope lock their horns. Male kudus lock their spiral horns and push against each other until one gives up. Impalas approach each other slowly. At the nod of the head or the roll of the eyes they rush forward and clash horns.

CREATURE PROFILE

Common name:	Giant eland
Scientific name:	*Taurotragus derbianus*
Found in:	Many parts of Africa, especially Sudan, Senegal and Central African Republic
Height:	4.9–5.7 feet (1.5–1.75 cm) at the shoulder
Weight:	1,100–1,900 pounds (500–900 kg)
Feed on:	Grass, leaves and branches
Enemies:	Humans. Elands are killed for their skin and meat.
Status:	Endangered

WILDEBEEST

The wildebeest is a large hooved mammal found only in Africa. It is also known as gnu. There are two species of wildebeest, the black wildebeest, or white-tailed gnu, and the blue wildebeest, also known as the brindled gnu.

This is a herd of blue wildebeest.

Blue wildebeest

Of the two types of wildebeest the blue wildebeest is larger and more common. It has a boxlike head with large, curving horns that expand sideways, similar to cows, and a stiff black mane. Both male and female wildebeest have horns. Its light gray to bluish-gray color gives the species its name. Dark brown stripes run down the neck to the middle of its body.

The black wildebeest has a blackish-brown body.

Black wildebeest

This species is endemic to savannahs of southern Africa. It has a dark brown to black body. Its distinguishing feature is its distinctive white tail and the shape of its horns. Its horns expand forward towards its face and then curve upwards in a *U* shape. It has a bristly mane that is cream to white and black at the tips.

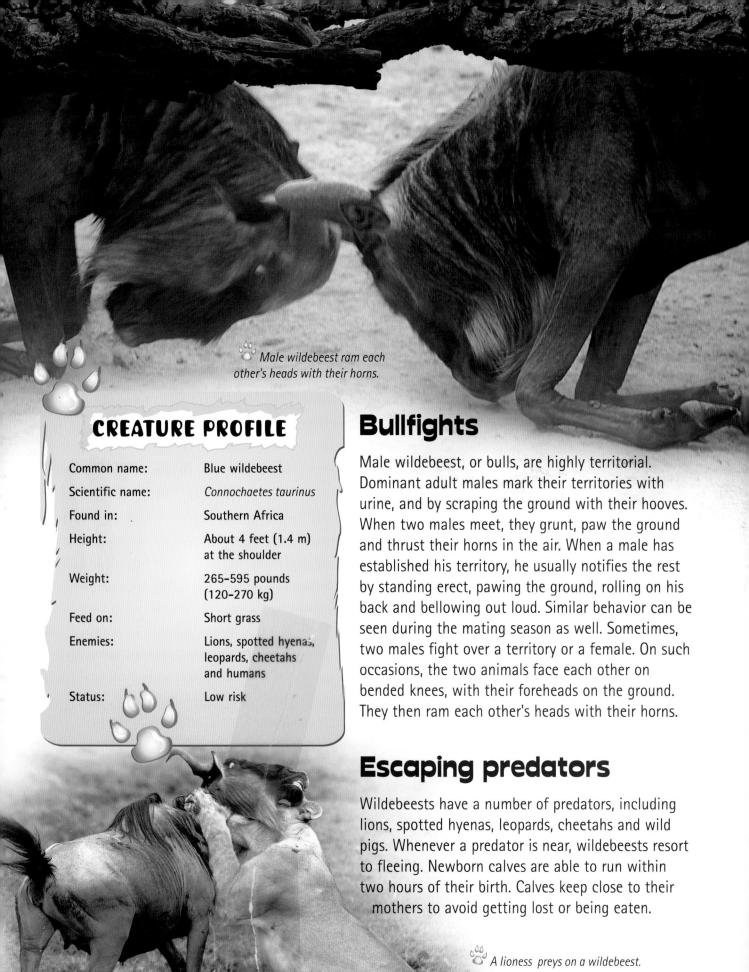

Male wildebeest ram each other's heads with their horns.

CREATURE PROFILE

Common name:	Blue wildebeest
Scientific name:	*Connochaetes taurinus*
Found in:	Southern Africa
Height:	About 4 feet (1.4 m) at the shoulder
Weight:	265–595 pounds (120–270 kg)
Feed on:	Short grass
Enemies:	Lions, spotted hyenas, leopards, cheetahs and humans
Status:	Low risk

Bullfights

Male wildebeest, or bulls, are highly territorial. Dominant adult males mark their territories with urine, and by scraping the ground with their hooves. When two males meet, they grunt, paw the ground and thrust their horns in the air. When a male has established his territory, he usually notifies the rest by standing erect, pawing the ground, rolling on his back and bellowing out loud. Similar behavior can be seen during the mating season as well. Sometimes, two males fight over a territory or a female. On such occasions, the two animals face each other on bended knees, with their foreheads on the ground. They then ram each other's heads with their horns.

Escaping predators

Wildebeests have a number of predators, including lions, spotted hyenas, leopards, cheetahs and wild pigs. Whenever a predator is near, wildebeests resort to fleeing. Newborn calves are able to run within two hours of their birth. Calves keep close to their mothers to avoid getting lost or being eaten.

A lioness preys on a wildebeest.

ZEBRA

Zebras are horselike animals with black and white stripes on their bodies. There are three main types of zebra, plains, mountain and Grevy's zebra. They are found in various parts of Africa. The black and white stripes act as a camouflage.

Coat of many patterns

The stripes vary with each species of zebra. The mountain zebra has a white belly with black stripes that are narrower than those of a plains zebra. The stripes on the plains zebra bend backward toward the rump to form a *Y* shape on its flanks. The Grevy's zebra, the largest of all zebra species, has an erect, stiff mane, longer than the mane of any other species. The stripes on the Grevy's zebra are narrower and more closely set and do not extend to the belly. The stripes form a gleaming white patch of white on either side of the tail. The stripes also vary with each individual.

Every zebra has a unique pattern on its coat, just like human fingerprints.

A herd's life

There is safety in numbers. Zebras know this fact very well and therefore always live in herds.

Zebras form small herds of about 20 individuals. A male zebra leads the herd. There may be two adult male zebras in a herd, but only one of them is dominant. The stallion usually stays at the back of the herd to protect the rest of the members from predators. Mares remain with the herd for life, while foals leave the herd once they are old enough to start a herd of their own.

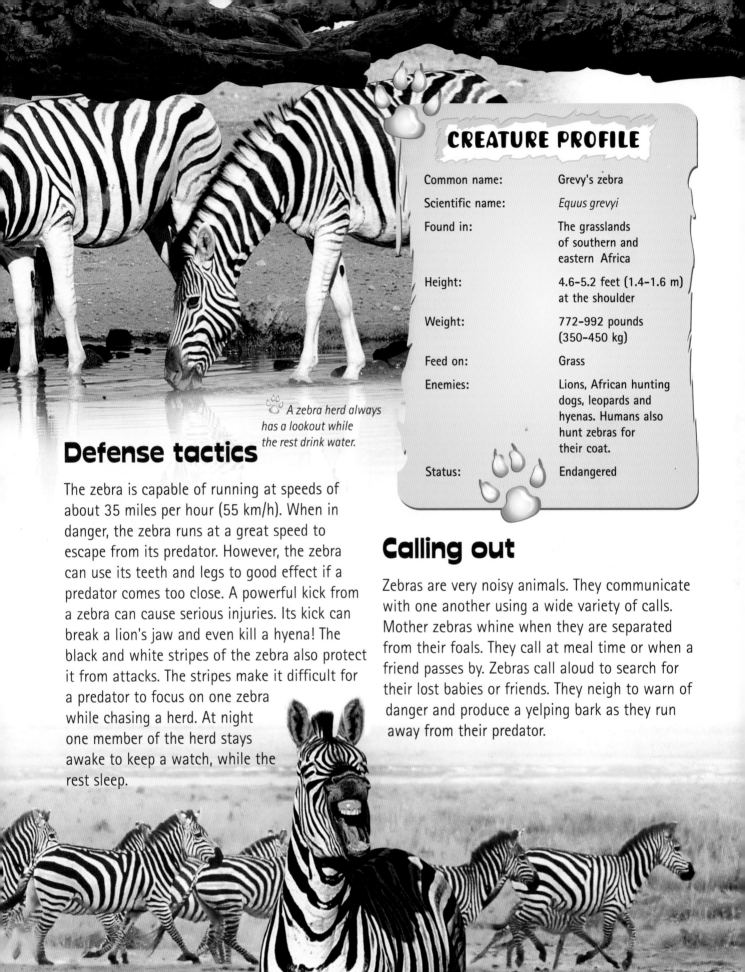

CREATURE PROFILE

Common name:	Grevy's zebra
Scientific name:	*Equus grevyi*
Found in:	The grasslands of southern and eastern Africa
Height:	4.6–5.2 feet (1.4–1.6 m) at the shoulder
Weight:	772–992 pounds (350–450 kg)
Feed on:	Grass
Enemies:	Lions, African hunting dogs, leopards and hyenas. Humans also hunt zebras for their coat.
Status:	Endangered

A zebra herd always has a lookout while the rest drink water.

Defense tactics

The zebra is capable of running at speeds of about 35 miles per hour (55 km/h). When in danger, the zebra runs at a great speed to escape from its predator. However, the zebra can use its teeth and legs to good effect if a predator comes too close. A powerful kick from a zebra can cause serious injuries. Its kick can break a lion's jaw and even kill a hyena! The black and white stripes of the zebra also protect it from attacks. The stripes make it difficult for a predator to focus on one zebra while chasing a herd. At night one member of the herd stays awake to keep a watch, while the rest sleep.

Calling out

Zebras are very noisy animals. They communicate with one another using a wide variety of calls. Mother zebras whine when they are separated from their foals. They call at meal time or when a friend passes by. Zebras call aloud to search for their lost babies or friends. They neigh to warn of danger and produce a yelping bark as they run away from their predator.

GIRAFFE

The giraffe is the tallest animal on land. It can grow to a height of about 18 feet (5.5 m). The giraffe is famous for its extra long legs and neck. This amazing hooved mammal is found in eastern and southern Africa. In particular many of them are found in two countries — Angola and Zambia. They like to roam about the savannahs and open woodlands.

Reaching up

The giraffe's neck alone is 6 feet (1.8 m) long. That is the height of an adult human being! A giraffe has only seven vertebrae, or bones in its neck. That is as many as humans have. But a giraffe's vertebrae are much longer and are separated by highly flexible joints. Its long neck helps the giraffe to reach up and pluck leaves from higher branches of trees.

The giraffe's tongue has special protection against the acacia thorns.

A thorny diet

A giraffe eats a lot to have energy for its daily routine. An adult giraffe can eat more than 132 pounds (60 kg) of leaves every day. Although a giraffe can eat any kind of vegetation, its favorite food is the leaves of the thorny acacia tree. The long thorns of the acacia stop most animals from eating its leaves, but not the giraffe! Its tongue, about 18 inches (45 cm) long, is covered with small bumps called papillae that protect it from the thorns. The giraffe's mouth also produces thick, sticky saliva that coats the thorns that may be swallowed by accident.

Only the giraffe can reach the tops of the acacia trees on the savannah from a standing position on the ground.

Giraffe movements

The body of the giraffe may be shorter than other hooved animals, but its long legs more than make up for this shortcoming. The front legs are slightly longer than the hind legs. A giraffe has a peculiar way of walking. It moves both the front and back legs on one side of the body together, followed by the legs on the other side. This movement is called pacing. While running the front legs move forward first, followed by the back legs. A giraffe can run at speeds of about 30 miles per hour (48 km/h). It also swings its back legs up, putting them ahead of the front feet, which is bent from the knee. The neck moves to and fro, so that the animal does not tip over while running.

Giraffes have distinctive ways of walking, running and even drinking water!

On the defense

The giraffe has a pair of bony horns covered with skin. These horns, called ossicones, have a tuft of black hair at the ends. Male giraffes use their ossicones to fight one another during the mating season. The ossicones are also used to defend the young from predators. However, a giraffe will more often use its legs to deliver a deadly kick during such occasions. The spotted pattern of its coat provides the animal with a good camouflage, making it look like a dead tree.

The horns of the giraffe come in most useful during the mating season.

CREATURE PROFILE

Common name:	Giraffe
Scientific name:	*Giraffa camelopardalis*
Found in:	Parts of Africa
Height:	Adult male: up to 18 feet (5.5 m)
	Adult female: up to 14 feet (4.3 m)
Tail length:	8 feet (2.4 m)
Feed on:	Leaves of the acacia and other trees
Enemies:	Young giraffes fall prey to lions, crocodiles, leopards and hyenas. Humans also hunt giraffes for their coat, meat and tails.
Status:	Low risk. Giraffe populations are stable.

HYENA

The hyena is the most commonly found carnivore in the African savannahs. There are four different types of hyena: aardwolf, spotted, striped and brown hyena. Of these, the spotted hyena is the best known and most abundant species.

Hyena facts

Hyenas can be light to dark brown or even gray, depending upon the species. They have compact bodies with small heads. Their jaws are powerful enough to crush even the largest of bones. Their front legs are longer than the back legs. Hyenas are very intelligent and this can be seen in their unique hunting tactics. Contrary to popular belief, not all hyenas are scavengers. The brown and striped hyenas are the true scavengers of the family. The spotted hyena is an aggressive hunter, while the aardwolf feeds on insects.

Living in clans

Spotted hyenas live in large clans of up to a hundred individuals. A dominant female leads the clan. Unlike many other animals, the female hyena is bigger than the male. The clan size depends on the availability of prey. The larger the number of prey, the bigger the clan is. Hyenas are extremely territorial and can get very aggressive and ferocious while defending their territory.

Spotted hyena hunt prey to a greater extent than the other hyena species.

Hyena cubs stay close to their dens so that they can run to safety in case of danger.

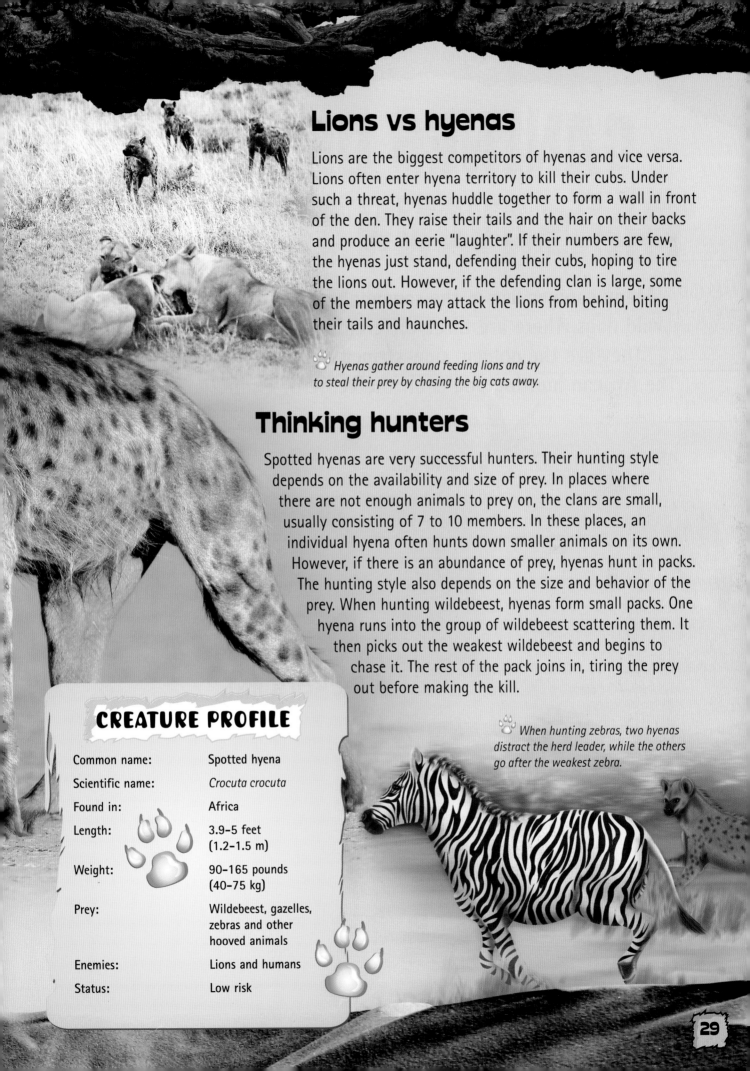

Lions vs hyenas

Lions are the biggest competitors of hyenas and vice versa. Lions often enter hyena territory to kill their cubs. Under such a threat, hyenas huddle together to form a wall in front of the den. They raise their tails and the hair on their backs and produce an eerie "laughter". If their numbers are few, the hyenas just stand, defending their cubs, hoping to tire the lions out. However, if the defending clan is large, some of the members may attack the lions from behind, biting their tails and haunches.

Hyenas gather around feeding lions and try to steal their prey by chasing the big cats away.

Thinking hunters

Spotted hyenas are very successful hunters. Their hunting style depends on the availability and size of prey. In places where there are not enough animals to prey on, the clans are small, usually consisting of 7 to 10 members. In these places, an individual hyena often hunts down smaller animals on its own. However, if there is an abundance of prey, hyenas hunt in packs. The hunting style also depends on the size and behavior of the prey. When hunting wildebeest, hyenas form small packs. One hyena runs into the group of wildebeest scattering them. It then picks out the weakest wildebeest and begins to chase it. The rest of the pack joins in, tiring the prey out before making the kill.

When hunting zebras, two hyenas distract the herd leader, while the others go after the weakest zebra.

CREATURE PROFILE

Common name:	Spotted hyena
Scientific name:	*Crocuta crocuta*
Found in:	Africa
Length:	3.9–5 feet (1.2–1.5 m)
Weight:	90–165 pounds (40–75 kg)
Prey:	Wildebeest, gazelles, zebras and other hooved animals
Enemies:	Lions and humans
Status:	Low risk

CANINES OF THE SAVANNAHS

This is a pair of side-striped jackals.

Many canines live in the savannahs. These include jackals and wild dogs. There are three different species of jackals in Africa. They are the golden, side-striped and black-backed jackals. The African hunting dog is on the verge of extinction.

Jackal

All jackals have doglike features and a bushy tail. They have long legs with blunt feet that help them to run long distances. They are nocturnal animals, active during dawn and dusk. The species differ from one another mainly in color. The golden jackal is sandy brown, while the side-striped jackal has black and white stripes along the sides of its body.

Here is the golden jackal.

The black-backed jackal is rust colored with a patch of black hair on its back.

A jackal's life

Jackals usually live in pairs or small packs of about six individuals, but single jackals can also be seen. A pack usually consists of a male, a female and their young. Male and female jackals mate for life. Jackal pairs are highly territorial. Both female and male jackals defend their territories fiercely. Jackals communicate with one another using yipping calls. Members of a family only respond to the calls of their own family. They usually ignore the calls of other families or individuals. Although they are known to be scavengers, these animals are excellent hunters.

Jackals are extremely cunning and agile.

Common name:	African hunting dog
Scientific name:	*Lycaon pictus*
Found in:	Africa
Height:	24–30 inches (60–76 cm)
Weight:	55–70 pounds (25–32 kg)
Prey:	Impalas, gazelles, warthogs, rats and birds
Enemies:	Humans. African hunting digs are killed, because they are dangerous to livestock.
Status:	Endangered. There are about 5,600 hunting dogs in the wild.

 The African hunting dog is on the verge of extinction.

African hunting dog

The African hunting dog is a very intelligent animal. This canine has long legs with four toes on each foot. The most distinguishing feature of a hunting dog is its colorful coat and large batlike ears. It also has powerful jaws that can tear even the thickest hide. Hunting dogs usually form packs of 6 to 20 individuals. The pack consists of a main breeding pair and several nonbreeding adult male helpers. Unlike many other herding animals, the female dogs leave the pack when they are mature.

Excellent hunters

African hunting dogs are most efficient hunters. They have the highest success rate in hunting among the carnivores. Before starting a hunt, the members of the pack take part in an elaborate ritual, by walking through the pack and touching and calling out to other members. During hunting, some of the members run close to the prey, while the rest of the pack follows at a distance. When the first hunting pack tires the one behind takes over. This technique is called relay hunting.

BABOON

Baboons are one of the largest species of monkeys in the world. These ground-dwelling monkeys are very common throughout Africa. There are five main types of baboons. They are olive, chacma, guinea, yellow and hamadryas baboons. Except for the hamadryas baboons, the rest are collectively known as savannah baboons.

Like all primates, baboon mothers are fiercely protective of their babies.

Common features

All baboons have a long muzzle that looks like the muzzle of a dog. Their eyes are set close to each other and they have powerful jaws. The body is covered with thick fur. Baboons have rough skin on their bottoms. These hairless pads of skin provide comfort while sitting. Both male and female baboons differ greatly in size and color. Males are larger than females.

The baboon's fur stands up when the animal is angry. This is enough to scare most other animals away.

Trooping in

Baboons live in groups known as troops. A typical troop consists of about 50 individuals, including about eight males and around twice the number of females and young. The savannah baboon troops are usually led by a dominant female. The males in a troop are often responsible for defending the troop members. The troop sleeps, travels and looks for food together. The members of a troop form strong bonds with one another through mutual grooming. This also helps keep the baboons clean and free of lice.

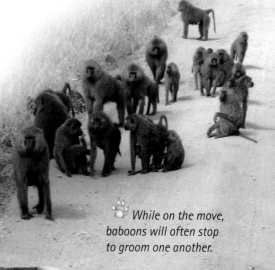

While on the move, baboons will often stop to groom one another.

Baboon behavior

Baboons are omnivorous. However, they prefer grass, berries, leaves, roots and bark. They forage for food through the day, often resting during the hottest part. Females carry their newborn in one hand, holding them close to the stomach while travelling. When the infant is about six weeks old, it lies on the back of its mother. Although it is the female who looks after the young, male baboons are known to help. They do so by gathering food for the young and even playing with them.

 Baboons can deliver nasty bites during a fight.

Hamadryas baboon

The hamadryas baboon is behaviorally and physically distinct from the savannah baboons, though it lives on the edge of the savannahs in Ethiopia and Somalia. Hamadryas baboons are also found in the Middle East, in Saudi Arabia and Yemen. The male of this species is noted for its distinctive silverish gray color and thick mane. The female is brown and without a mane. Both male and female have a pink face and bottom. This species has a complex social structure. An adult male dominates a group of about 10 females, known as his harem. Two or more harems constitute a clan. Several clans make a band and many bands put together form a troop. A large troop can have over 140 members!

CREATURE PROFILE

Common name:	Hamadryas baboon
Scientific name:	*Papio hamadryas*
Found in:	Africa and Arabia
Weight:	Adult males: 33–40 pounds (15–20 kg)
	Adult females: 19–27 pounds (8–13 kg)
Feed on:	Leaves, bark, nuts, berries, insects and flesh of small animals
Enemies:	Leopards, cheetahs and humans. Baboons are considered to be agricultural pests and are therefore killed in large numbers.
Status:	Listed as near threatened

OTHER MAMMALS

Apart from antelope, big cats, baboons and hunting dogs, the savannahs are home to a wide range of animals, some of which remain a relative mystery to us. Others, like vervet monkeys, servals, caracals, gazelles and warthogs, have names you might recognize but probably don't know much about.

Vervet monkeys

These small, black-faced monkeys are found in a variety of habitats outside rainforests. However, they prefer acacia woodlands bordering savannahs. Therefore, they stick to woodlands with streams or lakes nearby. Like all monkeys, vervet monkeys live in troops of 10 to 50 individuals. A troop mainly consists of adult females and the young. Adult males move in and out of these troops. The most unique behavior of vervet monkeys is the different calls they use to indicate different types of predators. When a member produces the eagle call, the rest of the troops hide among dense vegetation.

The vervet monkey calls out to alert the other monkeys when a predator is near.

Servals and caracals

Servals and caracals are species of wild cats that lead solitary, secretive lives. Both cats have small, slender bodies and long legs. Their heads are small with a long neck and large ears. The caracal has tufts of black hair at the top of its ears. Both servals and caracals hunt at night and therefore rely mainly on sound to locate their prey. Once the prey is located, the cat moves silently towards it and pounces on it. Servals often play with their victims before eating them. Caracals are known for their exceptional skill at bird hunting. They reach out and use their front paws to snatch a flying bird, and sometimes even more than one bird at a time.

Here are a caracal (left) and a serval (right).

Warthogs

The warthog is the only wild pig that is able to live in the dry savannah. A warthog has a large head with thick protective pads, or warts, on either side. Two large pairs of warts are located just below the eyes, and between the tusks and the eyes. The male warthog has two smaller warts on either side of its head. The warthog has an elongated snout with two pairs of tusks. A bristly mane extends from the top of the head to the middle of the back. A warthog family consists of a female and her young. Male warthogs live alone or in small bachelor groups. Males are not territorial, but they fight fiercely during the mating season.

The tusks of a warthog are dangerous weapons.

CREATURE PROFILE

Common name:	Warthog
Scientific name:	*Phacochoerus africanus*
Found in:	Africa
Length:	3–5 feet (1–1.5 m)
Weight:	110–330 pounds (50–150 kg)
Feed on:	Grass, bark, roots, berries, fruit, eggs, dead animals and small mammals, reptiles and birds
Enemies:	Lions, leopards, hyena and humans
Status:	Plentiful. There are plenty of warthogs in the wild.

VULTURE

Vultures are large birds of prey that feed on carcasses. It is because of this diet that these birds are known as scavengers. Although they are considered to be birds of prey, vultures rarely kill an animal on their own. Their feet are too weak and their claws too blunt to grasp live prey effectively.

Feeding on the dead

Vultures have many special features that are suited to their scavenging lifestyle. Their heads and sometimes even the necks lack feathers. This is a huge advantage, as vultures have to stick their heads into decaying carcasses. If the head and neck had feathers, they would become dirty and would be difficult to clean, leading to infections. Vultures also have excellent eyesight that helps them spot carcasses from a distance. Some vultures use their powerful beaks to rip the skin of the carcass.

Aided flight

Unlike most other flying birds, vultures have heavy bodies. They also have large, broad wings that help them lift their bodies into the air. However, most of the larger varieties also rely on hot air to aid them in flight. Vultures are usually found in dry, open lands. Air close to the ground in these regions rises as it heats up, creating thermals. A thermal is a bubble of hot air. Vultures glide around inside the rising bubble, using the hot air to hold them up.

Cracking the shell

Vultures feed mainly on carcasses. This does not mean that they do not hunt for food. Some of the larger species prey on young birds and small rodents. The palm-nut vulture feeds on oil palm nuts and shellfish. Some vultures hunt in shallow waters for fish. The most interesting hunting vulture is the Egyptian vulture. This species is known to crack open tough ostrich eggshells by either smashing the eggs against rocks or throwing stones on them. If no stone is available nearby, this vulture will even go in search of a stone. It will then carry the stone back in its beak and throw it at the egg with a lot of force.

Vultures often place their nests on the top branches of acacia trees.

Vultures feed on carcasses. Their rough tongues help vultures to pull flesh into the mouth.

Nature's waste managers!

Vultures are predominantly scavenger birds. They feed on dead bodies. They therefore play an important role in keeping the environment clean. If it were not for them, the dead bodies of animals would rot and pollute the environment. This would breed diseases and infections. Moreover, many leather tanners, craftsmen and bone collectors depend on the vultures to clean the carcasses for free!

OSTRICH

The ostrich is a flightless bird. It is the largest bird in the world. It makes up for its inability to fly by running at a speed that can reach 40 miles per hour (65 km/h). In fact, the ostrich is the fastest creature on two legs.

An ostrich can see a long distance even when it is sitting down.

Ostrich facts

The ostrich can grow up to an average height of 8 feet (2.4 m) and weighs between 198 and 300 pounds (90-135 kg). The adult male has mostly black feathers while the female and young male have grayish-brown feathers. The ostrich has strong legs. Each leg has two toes, one of which has a large claw. Like other birds, the ostrich does not have teeth, so it cannot chew its food. However, it compensates by swallowing small pebbles. These pebbles help to grind the food inside the stomach and help in digestion.

The ostrich is the largest bird.

The ostrich lacks teeth and so swallows pebbles to help grind the food in digestion.

Wings for all seasons

The wings of the ostrich might not help the bird fly, but they perform many other tasks. During mating displays, the male ostrich spreads its wings and engages in a peculiar courtship dance to impress the female. The wings are also used to provide shade to the eggs and, later on, the chicks. The soft feathers of the wings protect the bird from extreme weather conditions. In the summer, the bird fans itself with its wings. During the winter, it covers its bare legs with its wings to keep warm.

Safety measures

Ostriches have very long necks that help them detect danger from a long distance. Adult ostriches have very few enemies as they are aggressive and can deliver a fatal kick with their strong legs. Ostriches can also outrun most predators. However, the chicks often fall prey to predators such as jackals. The adult birds usually try to distract the predators with aggressive displays so that the chicks can escape during the confusion. The adults beat their wings and run up and down making loud noises. Sometimes they even sit on the ground and beat up a cloud of dust with their wings until the chicks are led to safety.

The only wild ostriches to be found now are in Africa.

CREATURE PROFILE

Common name:	Ostrich
Scientific name:	*Struthio camelus*
Found in:	Eastern and southern parts of Africa
Height:	7–9 feet (2.1–2.7 m)
Weight:	198–300 pounds (90–135 kg)
Feed on:	Fruit, seeds, leaves, insects, lizards and other small animals
Enemies:	Humans. Ostriches are targeted for their magnificent feathers.
Status:	Threatened

Moving together

Ostriches live in dry areas and move about in herds looking for food and water. A herd might consist of 5 to 50 individuals. Ostriches have also been known to travel with other grazing animals such as zebras. An ostrich herd can be led by either a male or a female. The leader of the herd chooses the grazing grounds and makes all decisions.

REPTILES OF THE SAVANNAH

Apart from the great variety of mammals and birds, the African savannahs have some of the world's largest and most interesting reptiles. These include a wide range of monitor lizards, snakes and the gigantic Nile crocodile.

The savannah monitor lizard is about 3.3 to 5 feet (1-1.5 m) long.

Monitor lizards

African savannahs are known for the large number of monitor lizards that live there. Of these, the savannah monitor is the most well known. This huge lizard has a stout body with a thick skin. It is easily identified by the unkeeled scales on the back of the neck that look like pimples. The savannah monitor's front legs have extremely sharp claws which are used for digging. It uses its longer rear legs for running. This lizard has a blue snakelike tongue. Its head can turn in all directions! Savannah monitors can expand their mouths, like snakes, to swallow larger prey. They usually feed on worms, insects, birds, small reptiles and rodents. They eat voraciously during the wet season so that they can go without food during the dry season.

Snakes

The best-known snakes of the savannahs include the black mamba and the rock python. The black mamba is the largest venomous snake in Africa. It can grow up to 14 feet (4.5 m) in length. It is also the world's fastest snake, known to reach speeds of about 12 miles per hour (20 km/h). Black mambas are ground-dwelling snakes and are found in open grasslands and rocky places. They are extremely poisonous and can kill an adult human with a single bite. The rock python is the longest of all African snakes. It can reach a length of 20 feet (6 m). The rock python is highly dependent on water and therefore hides in a deep burrow through the hottest parts of the summer.

Nile crocodile

The Nile crocodile is the largest of the three African crocodiles. An adult crocodile can grow up to 16 feet (5 m) long. This crocodile has a long snout and is olive green. Nile crocodiles live in freshwater swamps, rivers and lakes. These crocodiles are found only in the mainland of Africa and the island of Madagascar. Fish make up a major part of their diet. They also prey on bigger animals such as antelope, wild buffaloes and even big cats. The Nile crocodile usually hides underwater, waiting for prey to come to drink water. Only the eyes and snout of the crocodile can be seen above the water. When the prey is close enough, the crocodile grabs it with powerful jaws, dragging the prey into the water to drown it. Nile crocodiles also eat dead animals.

The teeth of Nile crocodiles are conical and help to grab and grip prey.

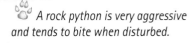
A rock python is very aggressive and tends to bite when disturbed.

CREATURE PROFILE

Common name:	Nile crocodile
Scientific name:	*Crocodylus niloticus*
Found in:	Mainland Africa, Madagascar
Length:	About 16 feet (5 m)
Weight:	About 990 pounds (450 kg)
Feed on:	Fish, antelope, zebras, rhinoceroses, buffalos, giraffe and big cats
Enemies:	Humans. Nile crocodiles were once hunted extensively for their hides. Strict environmental protection laws have, however, helped to revive their population.
Status:	Least concern. There are about 500,000 Nile crocodiles in the wild.

SAVANNAHS IN DANGER

The savannahs, and all the plants and animals living in them, are in grave danger of being wiped out. Human activities such as hunting, overgrazing and habitat destruction are the main threats to the survival of the savannahs.

Climatic changes

The Earth is warming up due partly, to increases in the number of factories, and large-scale deforestation. This increases the level of carbon dioxide in the atmosphere. This greenhouse gas traps the heat of the sun, thereby increasing the temperature. The rise in temperature in turn affects the distribution and abundance of plants and animals severely. In the already hot savannah region, the rise in the average temperature is resulting in the death of many animals. The raised temperature is also destroying several species of grass and shrubs found there. Rainfall is becoming more scarce in the savannahs, which is making it difficult for plants and animals to survive.

Habitat destruction

Over the last few decades, the number of people living in the savannahs has risen. This is a matter of concern as more and more land is being used up for housing and agriculture. Sometimes, they also cause fires that spread rapidly and destroy a large area of land. People also cut down the few trees that grow in the savannahs and use the wood as fuel or to build houses. This upsets the balance of nature as many animals depend on the trees for shade and food.

Overgrazing

People who live in the savannahs usually rear domestic animals such as cows and goats. These animals graze on the grass of the savannahs that is also the main diet of a large number of wild herbivores living there. This limits the food available to wild animals. Overgrazing forces many of the plant-eating animals, such as the antelope, to migrate in search of food. This unnatural migration often leads to their death. Wild animals also catch diseases from domestic animals. Many times, the wild animals are not able to fight these diseases and die. Sometimes, the disease may even spread and wipe out an entire group of animals.

The clearing of savannahs for domestic use and overgrazing by cattle have left the savannahs with reduced vegetation for the wild animals.

Illegal hunting

Hunting of animals is one of the biggest threats to the survival of savannah wildlife. People hunt animals for their meat, skin and horns. Elephants are hunted extensively for their tusks and rhinoceroses for their horns. This has led to a drastic decline in their populations. Although strict laws have been introduced to protect these animals, illegal hunting continues to threaten savannah wildlife. When there is a shortage of their prey in the wild, lions and leopards attack domestic animals. People living in the area then kill these wild animals. This is also a big reason for the dwindling number of savannah animals.

Illegal hunting for tusks, horns and fur of animals is driving them to the brink of extinction.

Glossary

Alert (uh-LERT) Careful

Ambush (AM-bush) To hide oneself and attack suddenly

Breed (BREED) To find a partner to produce a young one

Carcass (KAHR-kus) Dead body

Clash (KLASH) To crash together

Cloven (KLOH-ven) Split

Distract (dih-STRAKT) To draw someone's attention away from something

Diurnal (dy-UR-nul) To be active during day time

Endemic (en-DEH-mik) Living in a particular region

Fatal (FAY-tul) Causing death

Forage (FOR-ij) To search for food

Gemsbok (GEMZ-bahk) A species of antelope

Grave (GRAYV) Serious

Grooming (GROOM-ing) To clean one another

Harem (HER-em) A group of female partners for a male

Haunches (HONCH-ez) The hip and the buttock

Incisor (in-SY-zur) Tooth located in the front, used for cutting

Predator (PREH-duh-ter) One who hunts and kills animals for food

Glossary

Prehensile (pree-HENT-sul) Adapted for grasping

Primate (PRY-mayt) Order of intelligent mammals that includes monkeys, apes and humans

Rosettes (roh-ZETS) Ringlike spots on the body of animals like jaguars and leopards

Scavengers (SKA-ven-jerz) Animals that eat dead bodies

Slender (SLEN-der) Delicate and thin

Solitary (SAH-luh-ter-ee) Alone

Sprint (SPRINT) A burst of speed

Stalk (STOK) To chase prey

Stealth (STELTH) Approaching prey silently

Submerged (sub-MERGD) To remain underwater

Teeming (TEEM-ing) To be full of things

Territorial (ter-uh-TOR-ee-ul) To defend one's territory or area

Wander (WON-der) To move about

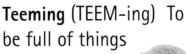

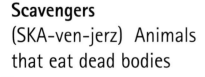

Further Reading & Web Sites

Guimbly, Shona. *Zebras*. Salt Lake City, Utah: Benchmark Books, 1999.

Leach, Michael. *Hippopotamus*. New York: Harcourt, 2000.

Thompson, Gare. *Serengeti Journey: On Safari in Africa*. Des Moines, Iowa: National Geographic Society, 2006.

Winner, Cherie. *Lions*. Minnetonka, MN: T&N Children's Publishing, 2001.

Due to the changing nature of Internet links, PowerKids Press has developed an online list of Web sites related to the subject of this book. This site is updated regularly. Please use this link to access the list: www.powerkidslinks.com/wcre/safari/

Index

Index